WARRIORS, WIGMEN, AND THE CROCODILE PEOPLE

JOURNEYS IN PAPUA NEW GUINEA

BARBARA A. MARGOLIES

Four Winds Press ❋ *New York*

Maxwell Macmillan Canada *Toronto* Maxwell Macmillan International *New York* *Oxford* *Singapore* *Sydney*

For Ira, Ilisa, and Gregory— B.A.M.

Afoot and light-hearted I take to the open road,
Healthy, free, the world before me,
The long brown path before me leading wherever I choose.
(from "Song of the Open Road" by Walt Whitman)

Sincere thanks to His Excellency, Ambassador Renagi R. Lohia, for reading my manuscript, for sharing his country, and for delighting me with the entrancing legends of Papua New Guinea.

—B.A.M.

Library of Congress Cataloging-in-Publication Data Margolies, Barbara, A., date. Warriors, Wigmen, and the Crocodile People: Journeys in Papua New Guinea / by Barbara A. Margolies.—1st ed.   p.   cm. Summary: Visits two different communities on the South Pacific island of Papua New Guinea and describes their traditional ways of life. ISBN 0-02-762283-5 1. Huli (Papua New Guinea people)— Social life and customs—Juvenile literature. 2. Ethnology—New Guinea— Sepik River Valley—Juvenile Literature. 3. Papua New Guinea—Social life and customs—Juvenile literature. 4. Sepik River Valley (New Guinea)—Social life and customs—Juvenile literature. [1. Papua New Guinea—Social life and customs. 2. Family life—Papua New Guinea.] I. Title. DU740.42.M37 1993 306.4'099575—dc20 92-27475

INTRODUCTION

Papua New Guinea is located north of Australia, southeast of the Philippines, east of Indonesia, and west of other Melanesian islands, including the Solomon Islands. Papua New Guinea is made up of over 600 islands. The mainland is on New Guinea, the world's second largest island. The western half of New Guinea, Irian Jaya, is part of Indonesia, and the eastern half is part of the independent state of Papua New Guinea.

During World War II, the Japanese invaded Papua New Guinea and established a strong position on New Britain, as well as in the northern part of the mainland. Allied forces—Americans, Australians, New Zealanders, and British—landed and fought fierce battles against the Japanese troops. Finally, by 1945, the Japanese retreated and surrendered.

Colonized by Britain and Germany and then administered jointly by Australia and the United Nations, Papua New Guinea became an independent state in 1975. The government is based on the British Westminster parliamentary system.

Papua New Guinea is home to about four million people, who share over 750 languages and dialects, according to their clans or tribal groups. The country is rich in diverse cultures and unique traditions.

Papua New Guinea is a land of high, rugged mountains and deep valleys, rivers surrounded by thick jungle, and mosquito-infested swamps.

As a developing nation, Papua New Guinea has incredible sources of natural wealth: the beautiful coral reefs off the coastal areas attract tourists and provide coral for jewelry; crocodiles are raised on farms for their skins; a huge logging industry offers rosewood, oak, kwila, ebony, and walnut. The forests and jungles are home to many species of birds of paradise, parrots, pigeons, kingfishers, and cassowaries. Besides farming vegetables and fruits for their own consumption, the people of Papua New Guinea grow coffee, tea, cocoa, spices, and copra for export. Fish are plentiful in the waters surrounding Papua New Guinea, and fish-processing plants are being developed. Gold and copper are mined, and oil is now exported to other countries.

These wonderful natural resources are quickly bringing economic growth, which in turn invites cultural change. But what will happen to the indigenous peoples and their traditions as outside influences sweep this beautiful land?

This book will show just two of the many communities in Papua New Guinea facing change today, the Hulis of the Southern Highlands and the people of the Sepik River.

NEW GUINEA

Indonesia

Australia

ADMIRALTY ISLANDS

MANUS ISLAND

NEW HANOVER

BISMARCK SEA

IRIAN JAYA

Kanganaman

Yentchan   Mindimbit

Sepik River

Palambei   Kaminibit

Aibom

Blackwater region

BISMARCK ARCHIPELAGO

southern highlands

Tari

Tari Valley

Mount Hagen

NEW BRITAIN

Mendi

TROBRIAND ISLANDS

GULF OF PAPUA

Port Moresby

D'ENTRECASTEAUX ISLANDS

PAPUA NEW GUINEA

CORAL SEA

PACIFIC
OCEAN

N

NEW IRELAND

BOUGAINVILLE ISLAND

SOLOMON SEA

MAY I WELCOME YOU to Papua New Guinea and to the pages of *Warriors, Wigmen, and the Crocodile People* by Barbara A. Margolies.

These rare glimpses at life in two distinct regions of Papua New Guinea offer a look at our varied traditions and values and a chance to meet the many diverse and wonderful people who call Papua New Guinea home. It is my hope that your journeys through this book will bring to you some new experiences and ideas and a desire to learn more about my country.

Renagi R. Lohia, OBE.
Ambassador
Permanent Representative
of Papua New Guinea
to the United Nations

Map by
Virginia Norey

SCALE

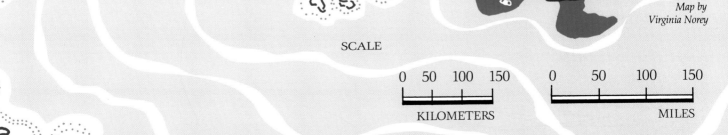

| 0 | 50 | 100 | 150 |
| KILOMETERS |

| 0 | 50 | 100 | 150 |
| MILES |

THE HULI PEOPLE

In the southern highlands of central Papua New Guinea is an isolated area called the Tari Valley. It is home to the Huli people, who continue to live much like their ancestors did hundreds and hundreds of years earlier.

In the 1930s the first outsiders, a group of Australian gold prospectors, visited the Tari Valley. The Huli people did not have any further contact with the outside world until the 1950s. Since then many things have changed—there are cars, trucks, bicycles, and occasional airplanes, schools, health clinics, and even western clothing. Yet some things have not changed at all.

LEFT: *A modern shovel, western belt, a key, and an umbrella are mixed with traditional Huli clothing.*

A Huli boy, Eiya, puts on his *arse-tanget*, a lap-lap apron, and a feather headpiece. He runs from his mother's house looking for Grandfather.

Today Grandfather has promised to show Eiya how to make a fire. Grandfather rubs wood and dry grass together to start his fire. Now Eiya does the same. He blows softly on the tiny fire, and smoke rises all around him. He did it! He made his own fire! Eiya is so happy and proud. And Grandfather is very pleased. He enjoys teaching Eiya the traditional ways of the Huli people.

ABOVE LEFT: *Grandfather's wig is made of his own hair and decorated with everlasting daisies and bird feathers.*

ABOVE CENTER AND RIGHT: *Eiya starts his first fire. Most Huli children learn how to start a fire in the traditional way.*

LEFT: *Eiya is dressed in the traditional male clothing of the Huli. His* lap-lap *apron was woven by his mother.*

LEFT: *Grandfather weaving a wall. The men teach the boys about Huli culture and traditions, and the women teach the girls.*

BELOW: *This house belongs to one of Grandfather's five wives. The roof is made of kunai grass. Every Huli wife must have her own house and garden.*

ABOVE: *Eiya's mother. Women decorate their faces but never as elaborately as the men.*

Next Grandfather shows Eiya how to weave the dried pandanus leaves into walls for a new house.

Soon Eiya will move to his father and grandfather's house. For now, because he is only six years old, Eiya still lives with his mother and sisters. It is Huli custom for men and women to live in separate houses.

Eiya is anxious to tell his mother about his wonderful morning. Mama is tending the mounds of sweet potatoes, the staple food of the Hulis. Mama also grows taro, bananas, and sugarcane. Men grow the same food, but in separate gardens from the women's.

After a short visit with Mama, Grandfather and Eiya go to check on the pigs.

When Huli children are very young, they learn that the pig is the most important possession of their family. A man's wealth and status in his clan is determined by the number of pigs he owns. Women and their daughters must take excellent care of the family pigs. And the pigs always live in the women's houses. Eiya's grandfather has so many pigs, though, he's had to build an extra house for them!

LEFT: *Eiya is wearing an* arse-tanget. *It is made of leaves from the tanget tree.*

BELOW: *Grandfather's pig house. After checking on the pigs, Grandfather will show Eiya how to use the bow and arrow. Grandfather will make Eiya a small bow that he can handle.*

12

Grandfather's brother, Waya, lives across the road. While Waya and his friends sit and talk in the garden, his sixteen-year-old daughter, Wanima, cares for the pigs.

ABOVE: *Waya and his friends. Later they will prepare and cook their own food. The Huli men and women never eat together.*

LEFT: *Uncle Waya and Wanima. Uncle Waya's pig is "helping" him garden by digging holes for plants. During special celebrations, many pigs are slaughtered and eaten.*

Wanima also must teach her younger sister how to make the traditional grass skirts and how to weave bilum bags. The bilum is a net bag that every Huli carries. The women's bilum is much larger than the men's, so the women can carry their babies or even piglets inside the bag!

Instead of taking care of the pigs and her sisters, Wanima would much rather be in school, learning to read and write. But like many other Hulis in the Tari Valley, her father cannot afford the school fees. She wonders if she will ever be able to travel to a big city if she can't read signs.

Waya brings food to his elderly cousin Haralu. The old man is blind. He likes to come out of his smoke-filled house and sit in the warm sunlight every afternoon. Caring for older family members is a very important Huli tradition.

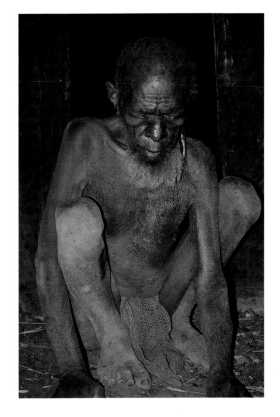

LEFT: *Wanima, her sister, and her brother. Huli women wrap their bilums around their heads, while the men wear them over their shoulders.*

RIGHT: *Because Haralu sits close to the fire to keep warm, he is always covered with ash.*

Back at Grandfather's house, friends have come to visit. Many Huli men still take great care in decorating their faces with paint. They show Eiya how it is done.

These days the men can buy paint in the market. Years ago they used ochre from the earth or vegetable juice to paint their bodies. Now they have brushes; before they used feathers.

While the men smoke and talk, Eiya thinks about his cousins Erowa and Tumba. A year ago they left their farm, walked for miles, and crossed many vine bridges to get to a faraway, isolated village where only unmarried men can go.

LEFT: *Unlike the everyday wig, this specially shaped wig is worn for ceremonies.*

TOP RIGHT: *Vine and log bridges are used throughout the highlands to cross deep ravines and rushing waters. Even pigs can walk across these bridges!*

BOTTOM RIGHT: *This long, narrow entrance leads to the wig village called Kepia.*

Many Huli men wear wigs as part of their everyday dress. Erowa and Tumba wanted to grow their *own* hair for their wigs. In the special village, the two cousins learn the secret ways to make their hair grow longer. They constantly wet their hair with ceremonial water. When they sleep, they put wooden logs under their necks so that their growing hair won't touch anything. Besides growing their hair for the wigs, the young bachelors learn all the wonderful traditions of Huli men, including playing the pan-flute and decorating their wigs with flowers and bird feathers.

FAR LEFT: *Tumba wears a cassowary bird leg bone, sharpened for use as a weapon, tucked into his waistband. He wets his hair constantly with ceremonial water.*

FAR LEFT BELOW: *It will take Erowa and Tumba about eighteen months to grow full wigs.*

LEFT AND BELOW: *The bird of paradise, whose feathers cover these wigs, has become an endangered species. Now, instead of just using arrows, hunters also use guns to kill these beautiful birds. And as the rainforests are cut down, the natural habitat of the bird of paradise disappears.*

Suddenly Eiya hears shouting. He runs to the road. Men are running and yelling, holding bows and arrows and machetes! Eiya can tell from their painted faces and bodies that they are going to fight another clan!

The men are angry: Two pigs have been stolen. It is payback time for these Hulis. The men gather behind a house to discuss how they will attack.

Traditional warfare, or tribal fighting, is still a very big part of Huli culture. A tribal fight can start from an argument over land, or just because one pig has been stolen! Sometimes, a small fight grows into a clan war that involves one thousand Huli men! Eiya knows that when he grows up, he will fight, too. He is sure that he will be a brave Huli warrior.

TOP LEFT: *This warrior's helmet may have been traded with a worker from a nearby logging camp.*

BOTTOM LEFT: *Huli warriors run in formation, chasing the enemy clan into the forest.*

ABOVE: *These warriors are discussing their plan of attack.*

Eiya and his family continue to live in the traditional way of the Huli people. In time to come, as more and more western ideas, tools, and luxuries come to the Tari Valley, the customs of the Huli will disappear, slowly, and forever.

BELOW LEFT: *Grandfather wears a belt of pig's tails.*

BELOW RIGHT: *The Huli people honor their dead by painting the skulls and bones of their ancestors and keeping them in the family vault.*

BELOW: *Huli women and children gather together on the side of the road. Traders and missionaries have made western-style clothing available to many people.*

BELOW: *Huli women and children gather together on the side of the road. Traders and missionaries have made western-style clothing available to many people.*

ALONG THE SEPIK RIVER

Far, far away from the Hulis, in another part of Papua New Guinea, live the people of the Sepik River.

A long time ago, the Sepik people were mighty head-hunters and cannibals. Today they no longer fight one another—peace has finally come to the villages along the Sepik.

The scorching sun beats down on the muddy waters of the Sepik River. Birds sing from the tall trees of the thick jungle. Millions of insects fill the air with their strange sounds. Crocodiles slither off the banks into the cool waters. Saui, her brother, Sarawabe, and their mother are paddling their canoe toward the village of Kaminibit.

LEFT: *Saui, her mother, and her brother. Many river people stand while they paddle.*

Saui and her family have left their home in Yentchan and are going to visit Saui's Aunt Likia, Uncle Singet, and cousins Gemma, Dora, Wangi, and Katio. As they pass the villages of Palambei and Kanganaman, children wave. Saui's mother smiles, seeing the friendly faces. She remembers her childhood, when villagers were always fighting other villagers—with bows and poisoned arrows! Gliding past the thick bush and tall grasses, Mother warns Saui and her younger brother never to enter the jungle alone. They have already learned about the many snakes and wild pigs that can attack small children.

BELOW: *A young girl watches Saui's canoe from the water's edge. Many children along the river now wear western clothing.*

Boys yell and splash in the water. The noise chases away the crocodiles. Saui wishes she could jump in and play, too, but she must unload the boat first. Mother has brought gifts for her sister's family—a pot from Aibom, cloth from the market, and onions from their garden.

ABOVE: *Children play in the Blackwater River area. Decaying vegetation creates tannic acid, which causes the river water to appear black.*

RIGHT: *Saui's paddle is made of kwila wood.*

The Sepik River is beginning to rise from the rains. People must hurry and work in their gardens, harvesting the sweet potatoes, tomatoes, mangos, and watermelons before the grounds are flooded from the swollen river.

Throughout Kaminibit village and all the other villages along the Sepik River, children have many chores to do. Saui runs to greet her cousin Gemma, who is busy plucking feathers from a chicken. Gemma and her mother will cook the chicken later, in time for dinner with their guests.

Early in the morning Gemma and her brothers caught many fish. The fish are being steamed over a fire and will be eaten tomorrow. Gemma and her mother carefully wove the fishing nets that now hang in the sun to dry.

The staple diet in the village is fish and sago. Sago is a starch taken from inside the huge sago palm trees that grow in the swamps. The starch is used to make pancakes, puddings, and cereal. The children eat fish and sago every day!

TOP LEFT: *This chicken is still alive as Gemma plucks its feathers. Cooking fires are built in the spaces under the houses.*

TOP RIGHT: *Sepik houses do not have refrigeration, so most food must be eaten soon after it is picked or caught. These fish, however, are being steamed and dried and will keep for a few days.*

ABOVE: *Some canoes are so long that they can hold many, many people.*

FAR RIGHT: *Gemma's neighbor rests after working for hours on his canoe.*

Just like Saui and her family, who came to Kaminibit by canoe, everyone travels on the river. The Sepik River is their main "highway." Children learn how to swim and paddle a canoe when they are very young. Canoes are made of tree logs. It will take Gemma's neighbor only a few weeks to carve his canoe. The prow, or front of the canoe, will be shaped like a crocodile's head. For the people of the Sepik, this is a magical way of scaring off the *real* crocodiles, so that a canoe can travel safely through the water.

Saui sees Dora. She is her youngest cousin. Dora is seven years old and lives here with her family. Dora's house is built on stilts. When the river rises in the rainy season, the house stays dry. Now Dora can still play with all her friends under the house, away from the hot sun. Her father, Singet, uses this area, too, to carve his statues and masks. Dora's house is made of bark from the sago tree. She helped her parents collect sago leaves. After they were dried in the sun, Dora and her mother wove the leaves to make a thatched roof for their house.

Inside, Dora sleeps on a woven grass mat. In the night many mosquitoes buzz around her. Some mosquitoes carry the malaria disease, and Dora has been very sick with malaria. She is feeling better now and will be returning to school.

In Kaminibit Community School, Dora studies mathematics, geography, science, English, and Motu—the official language of Papua New Guinea. Science is Dora's best subject. She wants to be a nurse or a doctor when she grows up. Then she will be able to help other children when they become sick with malaria.

BELOW LEFT: *Dora's house. In the rainy season the river will rise to just under the floor.*

BELOW RIGHT: *A teacher in his classroom. Many of the village schools lack books and supplies.*

Perhaps what sets Papua New Guinea and especially the Sepik River area apart from other areas of the world are the beautiful and strange-looking carvings and masks that are created there. The Sepik people have always believed in magic and in spirits, both good and bad. These traditional beliefs are handed down from generation to generation through storytelling and the art of carving. Each mask or statue is said to carry a legend or a magic spirit within it!

ABOVE TOP: *This father has begun to teach his young sons the art of carving. Each village has its own style of carving.*

ABOVE: *This man, sitting under his house, carves a mask.*

RIGHT: *This is a dancing mask worn during special ceremonies.*

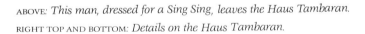

ABOVE: *This man, dressed for a Sing Sing, leaves the Haus Tambaran.*
RIGHT TOP AND BOTTOM: *Details on the Haus Tambaran.*

To house all the wonderful carvings, villagers build a Haus Tambaran, or spirit house. This is a place for spirits to live. Only men are allowed in the Haus Tambarans. The outside of a spirit house is often decorated with large masks or carvings called finials on the pointed roof.

It is in the Haus Tambarans that boys of fifteen or sixteen years old enter into manhood by participating in a skin-cutting ceremony. Cousins Katio and Wangi proudly show off their chests. Hundreds of small cuts have been made on their chests, shoulders, and backs. In the past, sharpened bamboo sticks were used to make the cuts, but razor blades were the cutting tools used on Katio and Wangi. While the boys were being cut, old men played on flutes. The music helped the young boys to think of something other than the pain of the razor.

Ash was rubbed into the cuts, and tree oil was applied to help their bodies to heal. It took weeks for the cuts to close. While the cuts were healing, the two boys remained in the Haus Tambaran. They learned their village traditions, tribal secrets, and stories. Along the Sepik it is said that the crocodile is the originator of earth itself and the creator of people. The Sepik River people are often referred to as the "crocodile people." Katio and Wangi are happy with the raised scar patterns, which look like the scales of the crocodile! When it was time for the young men to leave the Haus Tambaran, a huge Sing Sing was held in celebration of their manhood.

The Sing Sing is an important tradition of the Sepik people. It is a ceremony of dance and song that includes chants to chase away evil spirits or give thanks to good ones. The occasion for a Sing Sing could be a birth or death, a marriage or harvest, or even the welcoming of Saui, her brother, and mother as visitors to the village.

TOP LEFT: *Katio.*

BOTTOM LEFT: *Wangi.*

RIGHT: *During a Sing Sing, this dancer beats on his kunda drum.*

LEFT: *These men wear crescent-shaped necklaces called kina shells. Kina shells were once used as barter. Later Papua New Guinea named its currency kina.*

BELOW LEFT: *This woman has used the seed of the lipstick plant for the red stain that covers her face. The shells in her necklace come from the coastal area of Papua New Guinea.*

BELOW: *White egret feathers decorate this woman's headpiece.*

There always seems to be a reason for a Sing Sing! Men and women dress in the traditional way, with grass skirts, animal skins, and many bead and shell necklaces. Bird feathers are always used in the beautiful headpieces, since birds symbolize good luck and protection from the enemy.

The days are long and hot along the Sepik River. Night comes quickly. Fires are lit, and the family gathers together to eat and talk. In the quiet of the night, under a beautiful moonlit sky, children of the Sepik listen to magical stories about their ancestors.

At dawn tomorrow Saui, Sarawabe, and their mother will return to Yentchan. There is much harvesting and weaving to do, and Saui must be ready for school. But for now Saui will dream about the good spirits that will help bring them home safely.

A NOTE FROM THE AUTHOR

While traveling in Papua New Guinea, I had many exciting experiences, but one in particular was very, very special. News travels quickly along the river, and villagers always knew that I was coming. Up and down the Sepik, children were waiting as our small boat pulled up onto the muddy banks. In the village of Mindimbit, twelve-year-old Edna accompanied me as I explored, and spoke to me in perfect English. She carefully explained different customs of her people and answered the many questions I asked. She made me laugh as she helped me across the scary log bridges! When I was ready to leave, Edna asked if I would come back to Mindimbit on the way upriver. I promised I would, and a week later I returned. While other villagers stood around us, Edna shyly presented me with a bead necklace she had made just for me! It is one of the most beautiful gifts I have ever received, and I will treasure it always.

I thank Edna and all the wonderful children who helped to make my visit to Papua New Guinea so extraordinary.

—Barbara A. Margolies